SQUARE
ONE

◆

Steve Tesich

APPLAUSE
THEATRE BOOK PUBLISHERS

An Applause Original
SQUARE ONE
Copyright ©1990 by Applause Theatre Book Publishers

All inquiries concerning publication rights including book club, translation and anthology rights should be addressed to Applause Theatre Book Publishers, 211 W. 71st St., New York, NY 10023.

All inquiries concerning stock and amateur performing rights should be directed to Samuel French, Inc., 45 West 25th St., New York, NY 10010.

Inquiries concerning all other rights should be addressed to International Creative Management, Attn: Arlene Donovan, 40 West 57th St., New York, NY 10019.

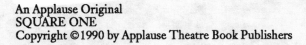

Library of Congress Cataloging-in-publication data:

Tesich, Steve.
    Square one / Steve Tesich.
       p.   cm.
    "An Applause original" -- Verso t.p.
    ISBN 1-55783-075-4 : $16.95 -- ISBN 1-55783-076-2 (pbk.) : $7.95
    I. Title
PS3570.E8S6   1990
812'.54--dc20   90-627
                                          CIP

APPLAUSE THEATRE BOOK PUBLISHERS
211 W. 71st Street
New York, NY 10023
212/595-4735

First Applause Printing, 1990

SQUARE ONE

"SQUARE ONE" was originally presented by **Second Stage Theatre** in association with **AT&T: OnStage** in New York City. The Play opened on February 22, 1990 with the following cast:

Dianne..**Dianne Wiest**
Adam ....**Richard Thomas**

Directed by **Jerry Zaks**

Set Design by **Tony Walton**
Lighting Design by **Paul Gallo**
Costume Design by **Ann Roth**

Artistic Directors: **Robyn Goodman** and **Carole Rothman**

CAST

Dianne

Adam

ACT ONE

Scene One

Dancing music is heard in the darkness. Lights up. Empty stage serves as our ballroom. Dianne *stands alone and perfectly still except for a part of her body reacting to the beat of the music. A Vienna Waltz. Enter* Adam. *Sees* Dianne. *Stops. Looks her over up and down. She feels observed. Turns her head. Sees him. Quickly turns away. He smiles. Strolls confidently and slowly toward her. Stops.*

Adam: Hello.

Dianne: Hello.

Adam: Would you like to dance?

Dianne: Yes, I would. Ever so much.

Gestures to start. She does not respond.

Dianne: I've always wanted to dance. *(Alluding to "other" couples dancing on the floor.)* They look so wonderful. The way they . . . The way their bodies . . . the way their feet . . .

Adam: Would you like to join them?

Dianne: Ever so much.

Gestures again to start. She does not respond.

Adam: Is something wrong?

Dianne: Yes.

He waits for a reply.

Adam: Well?

Dianne: I'm terrified.

Adam: Of dancing?

She nods. He smiles.

Don't be.

Dianne: Absolutely terrified.

Adam: There's nothing to it.

Dianne: Yes, there is. There's something to it. Do you think there's a chance, one in a million, one in a billion probably, but do you think there's a chance that if we danced we too would look like that and if somebody were watching us they too would say: Oh, look. Look at the two of them. Look at the way they . . . the way their arms . . .

Adam: I'm sure of it.

Dianne: Really?

Adam: Yes.

Dianne: Really and truly?

Adam: Yes, both.

Dianne: In that case, I'm all yours, Mister. Let's dance.

They dance. They look very nice doing it. Very romantic. They exit dancing.

Scene Two

A small table. Two chairs. Two drinks. Adam *and* Dianne *are sitting. There's a sense they've been sitting there a long time.*

Silent. Things are not going well. Adam lights a cigarette to have something to do.

Adam: Would you like another drink?

She smiles politely and shakes her head.

Would you like a club sandwich?

Ditto.

Would you like to go home?

She looks at her watch.

Dianne: Not yet.

Adam: Would you like me to go home?

She looks at him. Puzzled. Doesn't know what to make of this. Looks away. Silence and bad times resume. Adam looks at the menu. There are several pages.

Would you like a crême brulée?

Her face lights up. Can't believe her ears.

Dianne: Crême brulée? They have crême brulée here? Really? All my life I've . . .

She reaches for the menu. He stops her.

Adam: I'm sorry.

Dianne: Oh, I see.

Adam: I'm sorry.

Dianne: How could you?

Adam: It never occurred to me that you might believe me. Crême brulée? In this place?

Dianne: You have a cruel streak, don't you?

Adam: It was a joke. I was just kidding. Making small talk.

Dianne: That's what they all say.

Adam: I just can't understand it. We were having such a lovely time dancing, weren't we?

Dianne: Oh, yes. It was lovely.

Adam: And then we sit down here and you suddenly turn to stone.

Dianne: What do you expect me to do under the circumstances?

Adam: What circumstances?

Dianne: These circumstances. This. You and me. Sitting here. Over drinks. Getting to know each other.

Adam: It's the most natural thing in the world.

Dianne: Ha!

Adam: What's that supposed to mean?

Dianne: Don't tell me you're not terrified.

Adam: Of course I'm not terrified.

Dianne: Ha!

Adam: We're just sitting here talking.

Dianne: So you say.

Adam: But we were dancing. We were real close. You had your body right against mine. And we were talking while we danced.

Dianne: That was different. Music was playing. And we were dancing to the music. And when we talked, we were shouting above the music. "THIS IS WHAT I'M LIKE. THIS IS ME," I shouted above the music. "AND THIS IS WHAT I'M LIKE," you shouted above the music. And while we danced and the music played, that's what we were like. Now there is no music, is there?

Adam: No.

Dianne: We don't have to shout to be heard. We can hear every word we're saying.

Adam: You don't go out much, do you?

Dianne: What's that got to do with it?

Adam: This is the most natural thing in the world. There's nothing to it.

Dianne: Yes, there is. There's something to it. What do we do after we get to know each other? Let's say we somehow manage. Then what?

Adam: I don't know.

Dianne: And you tell me that's not terrifying. Ha! I don't know how much more of this I can take. I really don't.

Adam: Do you want to go home?

She looks at her watch.

Dianne: Not yet.

Adam: Do you want another drink?

She smiles and shakes her head.

They have wonderful club sandwiches here.

Dianne: *(Ditto. A beat and then a cry of yearning escapes her.)* I want a crême brulée! *(She almost weeps with yearning. Maybe she does weep.)*

Adam: I'm sorry. It was stupid of me.

She suddenly gathers herself. Stands up. Takes a huge breath. He stands up, thinking she's leaving. She sits down quickly. He sits down quickly. She stands up again just as quickly. He stands up, too.

Dianne: *(With a swagger.)* All right, Mister. Let's do it!

Adam: Meaning what?

Dianne: *(Cum swagger.)* Let's get to know one another over drinks once and for all.

Adam: Great.

Both sit down at the same time. At loss for words. Time marches on. Silence. Finally:

Dianne: This isn't as bad as I thought. *(Silence.)* How're we doing?

Adam: You're a nice looking woman.

Dianne: Thank you.

Adam: You're welcome. *(Beat.)* Very nice looking.

Dianne: Thank you very much.

Adam: You're very welcome.

Dianne: Where do you live?

He points.

Adam: Over there.

She's impressed.

Dianne: Really?

Adam: Yes. And you?

Dianne: *(She points.)* Over there.

Adam: *(He feels for her.)* I'm sorry.

Dianne: I'm used to it.

Adam: I don't suppose you live alone.

Dianne: Alone! Ha! *(She raises eight fingers.)*

Adam: There's eight of you?

Dianne: Not counting me.

Adam: Nine of you?

Dianne: Relatives. And at night when they start to scream, it sounds like there's a hundred of them.

Adam: Why do they scream?

Dianne: Nightmares. They wake up screaming.

Adam: They must be old.

Dianne: Very.

Adam: Yes. That explains it. The old ones tend to scream. They probably remember the bad old days before Reconstruction. Once they're gone, once that generation is gone, there'll be no more screaming. I believe in progress.

Dianne: I can see that. What do you do?

Adam: What do I do?

Dianne: Yes. Do you have a job or do you just have hobbies like the rest of us?

Adam: Do I have a job? Me? Are you kidding?

Dianne: I don't know. You take it anyway you want. I didn't mean to put any pressure on you.

Adam: You mean you don't recognize me?

Dianne: We're not old school friends, are we?

Adam: No.

Dianne: Thank God.

Adam: You don't have a television set, do you?

Dianne: Yes.

Adam: Then I don't understand it.

Dianne: What?

Adam: That you don't recognize me.

Dianne: You mean . . .

In awe. He enjoys her awe.

You mean to tell me I'm sitting here with . . .

He nods.

You're on television?

Adam: On Tuesdays and Thursdays.

Dianne: On prime days yet!

Adam: At nine o'clock.

Dianne: And at prime time!

Adam: The Patriotic Variety Hour.

Dianne: You're on the Patriotic Variety Hour!

Adam: Every Tuesday and Thursday.

Dianne: That explains it!

Adam: What?

Dianne: You're not going to be offended, are you, if I tell you something?

Adam: I'm far too secure.

Dianne: Good. Then I'll feel free. You see, my relatives, the really old ones . . .

Adam: The screamers?

Dianne: The very ones. They can't bear to watch the Patriotic Variety Hour.

Adam: Why not? It's a good show.

Dianne: They get confused. They think the show's a nightmare they're having and they start to scream, trying to wake themselves up, only they can't. I'm sorry. It's nothing personal, I'm sure.

Adam: Please. Think nothing of it. My own parents were the same way. They couldn't make the transition from the old to the new. That's why I had to move out. I live in my own apartment now.

Dianne: What do you mean?

Adam: I have my own place.

She is truly in awe.

Dianne: Your very own place?

Adam: My very own.

She stands up suddenly. He stands up, too.

Dianne: I'm sorry. I don't think I can take much more of this.

Adam: What's the matter?

Dianne: I know. I mean, I do know, this is what's done over drinks, but I can't take these fairy tales anymore. From start to finish. Everything you said. It's all been like so much crême brulée. I don't blame you, it's just that I can't . . .

She starts to leave. He grabs her arm. Holds her in place. Reaches in his wallet. Pulls out a plastic ID card with his picture on it. She looks. He kind of peeks over her shoulder, enjoying it all. She is stunned.

Adam: What does it say? Go ahead. Read it out loud.

Now that my blue days have passed,
Now that I've found you at last.
I'll be loving you, always
With a love that's true, always.

When the things you've planned
Need a helping hand,
I will understand, always, always.

Days may not be fair, always
That's when I'll be there, always
Not for just an hour,
Not for just a day,
Not for just a year,
But always.

He has a lovely voice. She's enchanted. When he finishes, she seems ready to applaud but is too moved to applaud and winds up holding her hands clasped across her breast.

Dianne: If I had any manners at all I would be speechless. Absolutely speechless.

Adam: Speaking of speechless . . . Seeing you there under the moonlight . . . What can I say?

Dianne: Are you still telling the truth?

Adam: Yes.

Dianne: The man just goes on. Could you please tell me. I don't mean to pry.

Adam: Anything you want.

Dianne: What's it like?

Adam: What's that?

Dianne: Your very own apartment.

Adam: It's a one and a half bedroom simplex overlooking the river. It has a built in . . .

Dianne: No, no. Not facts. The . . . the feeling.

Adam: Yes. I see. Well, I walk in and . . .

Dianne: Not so fast. Open the door.

Adam: Right. I take out my key . . . (*He takes it out of his pocket and kind of dangles it.*) I unlock the door. I open the door and walk inside.

Dianne: And there in front of your eyes . . .

Adam: And there in front of my eyes is my very own apartment. The things I left are still there where I left them. The thoughts I thought in the chair by the window overlooking the river are still there, waiting for me to think them again. The life I live, my very own life in my very own apartment, is waiting to be lived again.

Dianne: I knew it was like that. I just knew it. And nobody screams at night.

Adam: In my building? No. Every now and then, very rarely, but every now and then when the wind blows the wrong way from across the river I can hear the old people screaming in their quadrangles. Very faint, though.

Dianne *looks at her watch.*

Dianne: Thank you for sharing your apartment with me. And for telling me the truth. And for reminding me that there are happy truths in this world of ours.

Adam: We'll see each other again, won't we?

Dianne: We will?

Adam: I want to.

Dianne: You do? Really and truly?

Adam: Yes. Both.

Dianne: But I don't know what you see in me.

Adam: I see myself, of course.

Dianne: I have to tell you. I don't see myself in you.

Adam: You will.

Blackout.

Scene Three

A spotlight comes on. In the spotlight stands Adam in his Variety Hour outfit.

Adam: And now we come to the socially conscious portion of the Patriotic Variety Hour in which we try to salute segments of our society which are not normally given the recognition they deserve. Tonight it is my pleasure to "tip my hat" *(He does.)* and salute the disadvantaged and the devastated who're out there still giving it their best without any hope of getting anywhere. They may feel useless and forgotten but that's not the way we here on the Patriotic Variety Hour feel about them. We can still use them. And although we're aware as I'm sure all of you are that the very people we're saluting tonight are almost certainly not in a position to see this show, we here at P.V.H. feel that the show must go on. So, without any further ado, to those born on the wrong side of life, to the desperate, the lost, the cast-offs, to those who have gone from adolescence to obsolescence without a heartbeat in between, to those of you who will never hear this song, this song's for you. Maestro, if you please.

Music starts. Adam *sings:*

WHAT A WONDERFUL WORLD

I see trees of green,
Red roses too.
I see them bloom for me and for you,
And I think to myself
What a wonderful world.

I see skies of blue
And clouds of white,
The bright blessed day,
And the dark scared night,
And I think to myself
What a wonderful world.

The colors of the rainbow,
So pretty in the sky
Are also on the faces
Of people going by.

I see friends shakin' hands,
Saying "How do you do?"
They're really sayin'
"I love you."

I hear babies cry,
I watch them grow.
They'll learn much more
Than I'll ever know.
And I think to myself

What a wonderful world.

Yes, I think to myself
What a wonderful world.
What a wonderful world.
What a wonderful world.

Blackout.

Scene Four

The Park. A park bench. Enter Adam. *He's in a hurry. Stops next to the bench. Looks around. Takes out a sign from his jacket: "WET PAINT." Hangs sign on the bench. Looks around. Exits.*

Scene Five

Later. Enter Dianne. *Looking around. Sees the bench. Goes toward it. Ready to sit down. Sees the sign. Stops just in time. Stands there. Her weight on one foot. Then on the other. Looking around. Enter* Adam, *upstage with flowers in his hand. He sees her. She does not see him. He tiptoes toward her. She seems to be feeling something as she's looking out. Spins around and sees him. Applauds.*

Dianne: I saw you on the Patriotic Variety Hour last night. My relatives were screaming their heads off, but I didn't care. I saw the whole thing.

Adam: And?

Dianne: Bravo! Bravo!

Adam: You liked it, eh?

Dianne: I don't know if I liked it. But it was good. It was wonderful. You were brilliant. Brilliant.

Adam: Thank you.

Dianne: You are welcome.

He does a little dancing bit from the show. She recognizes it instantly and breaks up. He breaks out of the silliness and very meaningfully presents her with the flowers.

Adam: These are for you.

Dianne: For me? Whatever for?

Adam: Just for being who you are.

Dianne: And who's that?

He sits down on the bench. She tries to stop him but too late.

Dianne: Oh, no!

He turns and sees the "WET PAINT" sign. Flips it over. It now reads "DRY PAINT." He winks at her. She opens her mouth. Beginning to catch on.

You mean?

He nods.

Adam: Try finding an empty bench this time of day.

Dianne: So you?

Adam: That's right.

Dianne *leans back to look at him. Full of admiration.*

Dianne: You really are a rascal, aren't you?

Adam: What can I say?

He pats on the bench next to him. She looks around and with a kind of swaggering devil-may-care attitude, sits down next to him. A beat of just sitting there. Then she lets out a little squeal of joy. Covers her mouth.

Dianne: This is really something. It's prime park time and we've got a bench to ourselves. And people say nothing good ever happens on Wednesday. There goes that theory. It's even facing the sun. If I didn't know better I'd say life can be a real treat. Do you know what I mean?

Adam: I know exactly what you mean.

Dianne: Exactly?

He nods.

Dianne: Really?

He nods.

Well . . . in that case . . .

She sits back, crosses her legs in an almost reckless display of being at ease.

Adam: I'm so glad you liked the show.

Dianne: Oh, I don't know if I liked it. I never know if I like things. But I do know if it's good. It was better than good. And you . . . far be it from me to disagree with the experts who're in charge but as far as I'm concerned, you are better than an artist third class.

Adam: You really think so?

Dianne: I most certainly do.

Adam: I'm so glad you liked me.

Dianne: I don't know if I liked you at all, but you mark my words: You're somebody on his way up. And if someday, I don't know when, but if someday you're not an artist second class, I'll eat my hat.

Adam: Do you know how hard it is to become a second class artist?

Dianne: No, I don't.

Adam: Have you any idea of the kinds of things I have to do to be promoted?

Dianne: I don't have a clue. But you'll do them. You'll do whatever it takes.

Adam: I'm so happy that you have faith in me.

Dianne: I don't know if I have any faith in you at all, but I do know where you belong. Second class. Here. These are for you.

Hands him the flowers.

Adam: But I got them for you.

Dianne: Me? What did I do? You were wonderful.

Tosses the bouquet gently into his lap. He picks it up.

Adam: Thank you very much.

Dianne: You are very welcome.

A beat of silence. He has something on his mind. She is enjoying the sun.

If we stay here long enough, we're going to see a sunset.

He moves a little closer to her.

Adam: Do you want to get married?

She laughs, enjoying a good line, without changing her sunbathing pose. He looks at her and waits.

Dianne: Do I want to get married? (*Laughs again. She's having a wonderful time.*) You really are an entertainer.

He stands up. She looks at him. Stops laughing. Realizes.

Dianne: Don't tell me you were serious?

Adam: I was. Very.

She stands up.

Dianne: I didn't know. Sorry I laughed.

He's relieved by the explanation.

We better sit down.

Both sit down at the same time. Looking out, then at each other.

You can't be serious?

He fumbles in his pocket. Pulls out a little jewelry case. Hands it to her.

Adam: Here.

She's hesitant, but she takes it.

Go ahead. Open it.

She opens it. Screams.

Dianne: My God! It's a second key! *(Takes out the key on a chain from the case.)* You mean. Let me get this straight, Mister. You mean you are not just proposing a marriage, but a live-in marriage?

Adam: What do you think?

Dianne: I don't know what to think.

Adam: Personally I think live-in marriage is the only kind worth having.

Dianne: So do I, but . . .

Adam: But what?

Dianne: I appreciate the offer, Mister. You're the first person with his very own apartment who's ever asked me to marry him. I mean, I have been asked by other apartment owners but never to be a live-in wife. You're the first. And you'll always be the first. So don't think I don't appreciate the offer.

Adam: Are you saying, "No"?

Dianne: I don't know what I'm saying until I've said it. It's hard to think and talk at the same time. Most of the time I just think, you see. At home, relatives screaming, I just think. When the time comes for me to talk, it's almost never what I've been thinking about. The two are so separate. The Thinker me. And the Talker me. It's like one's a husband. And one's a wife. Only I haven't resolved which is which. I haven't resolved anything. Because? Because the Thinker thinks. And the Talker talks. But by definition, not to each other. You see what I mean?

Adam: I wish I could say "Yes".

Dianne: In a way, you see, I'm married already.

Adam: In what way would that be?

Dianne: In a way of speaking I'm married to myself. In a way of speaking I am my very own apartment which I share with my live-in husband or my live-in wife, I don't know which is which anymore, call it a spouse, call it my better half, call it what you will, but facts are facts and the fact is I'm stuck in this dead-end marriage of mine, trying to make a go of it but getting nowhere. We have yet to meet. Me and my better half. Yet to meet! Married to each other all these years, but yet to meet.

Adam: *(Interrupts.)* I wouldn't worry ab . . .

Dianne: I'M ON A ROLL HERE, YOU MIND?

Adam: Sorry. *(Gestures for her to continue.)*

Dianne: I guess what I'm trying to say, God knows I'm trying, what I'm trying to tell you is that in order to get married to you I would have to get a divorce first.

Adam: You mean from . . .

Dianne: From myself, yes. From, you know, call it what you will.

Adam: I think I'm beginning to . . . I wouldn't swear on it or anything like that, but I think I'm actually beginning to understand you.

Dianne: Nobody's ever told me that before.

Adam: You just haven't been around the right kind of people.

Dianne: You can say that again. Although, as far as being understood, I myself don't have a clue who the hell I am.

Adam: My point exactly.

Dianne: You mean I've been married to the wrong person all this time.

Adam: It's not for me to say.

Dianne: It's not an easy thing to say, but you might be right.

Adam: It happens.

Dianne: So you think I should cut my losses and give up on myself and marry you.

Adam: It's not for me to say. If you'd like to take some time and think it over.

Dianne: Are you crazy? That's the last thing I want to do in my condition. You're quite a guy, Mister. I hope you don't think I'm being coy. Playing hard to get.

Adam: Not while I've been here.

Dianne: But if we were to get married. How would we manage?

Adam: Manage?

Dianne: Yes. Manage on the little freedom we have. I mean, times being what they are, freedom just seems to slip through my fingers. No sooner do I get some then poof, it's gone. I don't know. All I know is the little freedom I have left at the end of the day, the take home freedom if you will, is hardly enough for one to get by on.

Adam: I think we can manage. How much freedom do

we need in the first place? Do you think that those who have more than we do are any happier than we are?

Dianne: I hope not.

Adam: They're not. And the little we have . . . well . . . what's the point of having it if you can't share it with someone?

She has to take a beat and think this one over.

Dianne: I've never thought about it like that. *(She smiles.)* That's a wonderful way of looking at it. I gotta tell you, Mister. If it weren't for the terror, I'd marry you on the spot.

Adam: Terror? What terror?

Dianne: The terror of two. The terror of trying to make a go of something with a stranger which was no go with myself. *(She finishes.)*

Adam: Let me see if I get this straight. If it weren't for the terror the idea of marriage would strike you as a viable proposition.

Dianne: And then some, yes.

He reacts like a man who's on top of things.

Adam: Lady, you just happen to be looking at an authority in terror.

Dianne: I'm all ears.

Adam: Think! What is the most terrifying profession you know of? Not one of the most terrifying, mind you, but the most terrifying. What is it?

She doesn't know. She bites her lip. She shrugs.

Think!

She thinks. She wracks her brain. She checks her watch and feels pressured by time.

Dianne: Could you give me a little hint?

Adam: No.

Dianne: Please!

He smiles, deciding to be generous. He does a little tap dance. Eureka, she's got it.

ENTERTAINER!

Adam *gestures to her that she's right.*

You're right! How right you are, Mister! I can't think of anything more terrifying than being an entertainer.

Adam: And yet there is one thing more terrifying than being an entertainer. And that is being an entertainer in our day and age. It's not like the old days anymore when an entertainer was an entertainer and the public was by God the public and the twain not only never met, nobody in his right mind wanted the twain to meet. But today! Today everybody thinks they're entertaining. They all go to those fun farms to work on their sense of humor and come back tanned and positive they're fun to be with. Check the Classified ads. The Personals. What do they all have, all those single white males and all those single white females, what do they all have, all claim to have in abundance? What?

Dianne: I don't know.

Adam: A sense of humor! I bet they do! Everybody thinks they can be an entertainer these days. And not just any old entertainer. Entertainer third class at least. What I'm saying is this. To be an entertainer these days, a state certified entertainer, a licensed professional, to have that be my bread and butter is to compete in a world that's laughing at its own material. So don't tell me about terror. I know terror. And I've learned to deal with it. And if I can do it you can do it. And if you can't do it, I'll teach you.

Dianne: Really?

Adam: And truly.

Dianne: I'm all ears.

Adam: Terror is a butterfly!

Dianne *hears*. Dianne *wants to understand*. Dianne *tries*. Dianne *gives up*.

Dianne: I don't get it.

Adam: Think!

Dianne *thinks. She wracks her brains.*

Dianne: I hate to make a habit of this, but could I have a little clue?

Adam: No.

Dianne: Please.

Adam: No.

Dianne: Last time. I promise.

Adam: Stomach. Stage fright. Butterflies. Terror.

Dianne: I get it. You get butterflies in your stomach.

Adam: That's right. And that's what I'm going to do to you.

Dianne: What's that?

Adam: Take all your terrors and make them fly away like butterflies.

He flaps his hands showing butterflies flying away. She follows their flight.

Dianne: How sweet. You really know how to sweep a girl off her feet, don't you?

Adam: What can I say?

Dianne: Mister?

Adam: Yes?

Dianne: Looks like you got yourself a wife.

She offers her hand. He his. They shake.

Congratulations.

Adam: You too. I hope we'll be very happy.

Dianne: So do I.

Blackout.

Scene Six

In the darkness, we hear "Here Comes the Bride" played on the piano but played in a way as if Beethoven had composed. Lights up on Adam's *apartment. All we need are the the absolute minimum impressionistic hints of that apartment. Several doors. Two chairs; one of them is a rocking chair. One of the doors opens. Enter* Adam, *carrying* Dianne *over the threshold. She's wearing her wedding gown and carrying the same bouquet we saw earlier in her hand.* Adam *is wearing a tux.* Dianne's *eyes are shut. The piano music, doing variations on the theme of "Here Comes the Bride", continues, but very softly.* Adam *places* Dianne *on the floor.*

Dianne: Can I open my eyes now?

Adam: Yes.

She opens her eyes. She looks left. Amazed. She looks right. Thrilled. She turns around, back to audience. Her arms go up in the air in ecstasy. Turns again facing the audience.

Dianne: I can't believe it. The view! The space! The color scheme! The lights! The small but personal decorating touches. The total look! That's the phrase I'm looking for. This apartment has a total look.

Adam: I'm so glad you like it.

Dianne: Oh, I don't know if I like it at all, but it's wonderful! Enchanting. Simply enchanting. A Paradise for two.

Adam: Thank you.

Dianne: Let me tell you something. You are welcome, Mister.

Adam: Do you think you can be happy here?

Dianne: Oh, let's not think about it. It's so big. *(She opens one door. Peeks in.)* Our bedroom! *(Opens another door.)* A tub! My God, it's a genuine sit-down tub. *(Tries* *another door. It won't open. So she moves to the last door. Opens it.)* A peek-in closet!

Adam: What do you think?

Dianne: I thought it'd be smaller. This looks bigger than one and a half bedroom.

Adam: It is bigger.

Dianne: I though you said you had a one and a half bedroom.

Adam: I did. But that was when I was single. I told you, didn't I, that this is state subsidized artists' housing.

She is full of admiration.

Dianne: Oh, yes. And it looks it. Third class all the way.

Adam: And when an artist of my rank gets married he moves up. This is, for your information, a full two-bedroom co-op.

Dianne: A two-bedroom! I've never seen a full two-bedroom co-op before. I've heard of them, but . . . No wonder it's so big. That explains it. *(But something troubles her. She's hesitant to mention it, but she does.)* Am I hearing things or do I hear music?

Adam: Oh, that's just the pianist downstairs. Concert soloist. Second Class!

Dianne: Really?

Adam: Yes. That's just his little way of welcoming you.

Dianne: Does he know me?

Adam: No, but he knows me and I know him. Everybody here is an artist.

Dianne: Really?

Adam: Yes.

Dianne: Except for me.

Adam: Except for you.

Piano stops. Dianne *looks around. Something is still troubling her.*

Dianne: Excuse me for asking. But are we going to sleep in separate bedrooms?

Adam: I hope not. I was kind of hoping we'd sleep in the same bedroom.

Dianne: Me, too. I mean, what's the point of having a live-in marriage in the first place if we're going to be by ourselves in separate bedrooms?

Adam: My sentiments exactly.

Dianne: But in that case, why do we need two bedrooms?

Adam: Never can tell.

Dianne: Never can tell?

Adam: That's what I said.

Dianne: Never can tell what?

Adam: When we might need it.

Dianne: When we might need it for what?

A beat.

Adam: Think of it as a guest room.

She looks at the door of the room. Looks at him.

Dianne: Are you expecting somebody?

Adam: No.

Dianne: Me neither.

Adam: Not yet.

Dianne: If not yet then when?

Adam: Never can tell.

Dianne: I see.

Walks away. Sits down in the rocking chair. Smells her bouquet. Adam sit down in the other chair. They look at each other. Smile. Adam takes out a cigarette. Sinks back in the chair. Lights it. Just as he's about to take the first puff Dianne is up like a shot. Runs to the door of the locked room. Gives a very strong pull and shake and before Adam can stop her the door opens. She goes inside. Light comes on. Adam waits outside. Nervous. Smoking. Pacing. A head of an extremely large stuffed animal emerges from the room. Then the rest of the animal. Then Dianne pushing it out. A huge animal with big eyes, silly grin. Dianne looks at Adam. Adam looks at her.

Dianne: A guest room? Is that what you said?

Adam: Yes.

Dianne *looks at the huge animal.*

Dianne: What kind of guests were you expecting?

Adam: Never can tell.

Dianne: I'll say. And what's this . . . *(Points to animal.)* Furniture? And where would the guest sleep? There's no bed in there.

Adam: Yes, there is.

Dianne: That's not a bed. That's a crib, Mister. And this is a toy. And that's not a guest room. That's a baby room.

Adam: It's all very simple.

Dianne: I'm all ears.

Adam: This is a state subsidized artists' housing co-operative.

Dianne: Yes, so?

Adam: When you get married you have to move to the married section of the complex. Which is where we are now.

Dianne: Enough facts. Get to the truth.

Adam: All apartments in the married section of the complex come with a spare room, a guest room, in the building handbook it's called "the future room."

Dianne: Oh, I see. It comes with the place.

Adam: The toys. The crib. Everything.

Dianne: So it's not your fault.

Adam: I should tell you something right up front because it might come up again and it's best to get these things settled at the very start. No matter what happens in our marriage I can promise you right now it will never be my fault.

Dianne: That's good to know. But I just don't know if I can take the pressure.

Adam: What pressure?

Dianne: The pressure to produce. And I'm not even an artist.

Adam: I wouldn't worry about it.

Dianne: I wouldn't either if I didn't feel the pressure. I don't do well under pressure. I find it hard to breathe. Whenever someone puts a gun to my head and says flourish or perish, I just . . .

Adam: Nobody's putting a gun to your head.

Dianne: It feels like a gun comes with this place.

Adam: If it'll reassure you in any way, I'll give you the facts again.

Dianne: I would prefer the truth instead.

Adam: The truth's up to you. All I can do is give you the facts and you can make of them whatever truth you want. Isn't that how it works?

Dianne: It's been a while since I've grappled with large concepts but I suppose you're right.

Adam: I'm not saying I'm right. I don't want to impose my standards on you. That's for you to decide. I guess all I'm really saying is you shouldn't put any pressure on your-self to "produce" as you call it. If it happens, it happens.

Dianne: When you get all this, the rooms, the views, the toys, aren't you expected to produce?

Adam: You're expected to try.

Dianne: I just don't see how we can manage to even try properly to say nothing of having one and raising one on the little freedom we have.

Adam: Maybe we have more freedom than you think. Maybe there is more to come.

Dianne: Excuse me for asking, but we are still talking about the baby, aren't we?

Adam: And all that it implies, yes. Our faith in the future. Our faith in each other. In our world. In ourselves. And all the rest.

Dianne: And what happens if we have one?

Adam: We fulfill our part and are fulfilled by it. We grow as human beings

Dianne: And who pays the price for all that growth?

Adam: Can't we talk about something else? *(Silence.)* Can't we change the subject? *(Silence.)* Can't we at least try to move on to something else? *(Silence.)*

Dianne: *(A beat.)* You know what can happen if we have a baby?

He gestures but does not answer.

You do know what can happen.

Adam: All I know is that no matter what happens it will never be my fault. And since we're both in this together, I would think the same applies to you. Coming to bed?

He starts to go. She doesn't follow. He stops.

Dianne: Here we are. You and me. We met by chance. We danced. A courtship followed. We got married. And now there's talk of having a little one. I think before we get any more deeply involved with each other there's something you should know about me.

Adam: What?

Dianne: I can only take so much. I hate to spring this on you like this, but it's true. My threshold, whatever they call it, is not very high. You see I understand, I have learned to understand, the need for the suffering of the old ones. For Reconstruction to work, the old ones have to be sacrificed.

Adam: There's no other way.

Dianne: I know that now. So when I walk past their quadrangles at night and hear them screaming, it helps to know that there's no other way, that it's necessary, and that it serves some ultimate good.

Adam: The past has to give way to the present.

Dianne: I've read those pamphlets and I tend to agree. But now there are rumors that the little ones might have to be sacrificed as well. They're already beginning to scream in certain neighborhoods. And nobody knows for sure if it's really necessary. If it really serves some greater good. I don't think I could take that kind of suffering.

Adam: You shouldn't underestimate yourself. None of us knows how much we can take. Coming to bed?

Dianne: Yes, but first I feel I must declare myself and take a stand on this issue.

He looks at his watch.

Adam: Go ahead.

Dianne: Summing up. With the old ones, the past has already been sacrificed for the sake of the future. If, as it appears, we might have to sacrifice that future, the little ones, we'd all be doomed to live in the present forever. And I couldn't take that. Therefore, with regret, but with conviction I refuse. Do you accept my refusal?

Adam: Sure. Coming to bed?

Blackout.

End of Act One.

ACT TWO

Scene One

In the darkness we hear a piano playing. It stops. Lights up. Their apartment. There are at least two more huge stuffed animals. They're all together in a tight group looking out, taking up enough space to form a room divider. Adam *is sitting in a chair reading a book.* Dianne *appears upstage with a bowl of popcorn. As she starts toward us we hear the piano again and either she's walking to the beat of the music or the music is mysteriously accompanying her. She becomes aware of it and stops. Music stops. Starts again. Different pace. Music starts and plays in step to the new rhythm. She stops. Music stops.*

Dianne: This is really annoying.

Adam looks up.

Adam: What?

Dianne: This music.

Adam *listens. Looks at her. She points downstairs.*

Adam: Did it happen again?

Dianne: Just now.

Adam: Those things happen.

Dianne: It's not the music. It's that I can't tell if I'm whatever you call it to the music or if the music is whatever that word is to me.

Adam: Accompanying.

Dianne: That's it. Watch. *(She starts to walk. No music.)* See what I mean? It's enough to drive you crazy. You never know when it's going to happen.

Adam: He's just practicing.

Dianne: But I'm not.

Adam: He's a renowned up-and-coming soloist. He's just rehearsing.

Dianne: But I'm not rehearsing anything.

Adam: So?

Dianne: But when the music, you know . . .

Adam: Accompanies.

Dianne: Right. It feels like I am rehearsing. Or it feels like somebody thinks I should be rehearsing something. *(Sits down.)* Want some popcorn?

Adam: No.

She eats some.

Dianne: You know what it really feels like. It feels like this whole artists' colony . . .

Adam: It's not a colony. It's a state subsidized artist co-operative.

Dianne: Fine. It feels like the whole state subsidized artist co-operative is sending me a message. Lady, you need help. Lady, nobody here knows what in the world you're doing or how in the world you manage or who in the world you are. So we're going to give you some music to fill out your character. That's what it feels like. And I resent it.

Adam: You wouldn't feel that way if you made friends with the other people here.

Dianne: They're all artists. They're not people.

Adam: It's an artists' co-operative. I told you that at the start.

Dianne: You didn't tell me they're all artists. Every one of them. The piano player's wife is a tragedian. I went down there to complain about his piano playing and this tragedian opens the door.

Adam: She's not just a tragedian. She's a second class tragedian.

Dianne: Fine. I wish her husband would accompany her and leave me alone. It's very intimidating . . . all this. (*She eats popcorn. Brilliant idea hits her. She beams full of herself and she announces to the world.*) Art intimidates life!

Adam: Imitates. Art imitates life.

Dianne *sits there, looking out eating her popcorn.* Adam *goes back to his book but not for long. Looks up at her.*

Adam: What're you going to do?

Dianne: I'm doing it.

Adam: You're going to eat popcorn?

Dianne: You want some?

Adam: No.

She sits there, eating popcorn, looking out. A contented spectator. The door to the baby room slowly creaks open and she slowly turns her head to look at it. Scrutinizes it. Looks at Adam.

Dianne: (*She looks up. She gestures toward the door.*) It did it again.

Adam: So shut it.

Dianne: I shut it a few minutes ago. We have to fix it.

Adam: We fixed it yesterday. How many times can I bother the maintenance bureau with our door.

Dianne: It's not fixed.

The door moves in and out, creaking open and shut.

Adam: We probably need a whole new door.

Dianne: Let's get a whole new door then. Take it out of my clothing allowance.

Adam: We can't do that.

Dianne: We can't?

Adam: Of course we can't. This is all original equipment. You just can't go around replacing things left and right without regard for the others.

Dianne: Why not?

Adam: Because this particular co-op has been granted landmark status.

Dianne: But it's a brand new hi-rise.

Adam: It's a brand new policy. The historical preservation people have been campaigning for more landmarks. This one was granted landmark status while it was still in the blueprint stage. It's the first place to be so honored.

He goes back to his book. The door keeps creaking in and out.

She tries to bear it. Can't.

Dianne: It really bothers me.

Adam: Then shut it.

Dianne: I just shut it a while ago.

Adam: Shut it again if it bothers you.

Dianne: It'll just "cr-e-e-e-a-k" open again. It's useless.
You do it.

Adam: What's the point if it's useless?

Dianne: The point is we're married.

Adam: So?

Dianne: The least we can do is take turns being useless.

Adam: It doesn't bother me.

*She tries to bear it. Looks at the moving door. Looks away.
Can't stand it. Jumps up out of chair.*

Dianne: Off I go again to shut the door that can't be
shut.

*Starts to go. Piano starts to play. She points across the vast
expanse of space from her to the door.*

Oh, no!

She sits down. The music stops. The door creaks on.

It's just enough to drive you crazy.

He jumps out of his chair.

Adam: All right already!

Throws book down. Marches past her to the door. Slams it shut. He marches back past her. Picks up his book. Opens the book. The door opens.

Dianne: And just think. This is still our honeymoon. The real hardball marriage is yet to begin. I have an idea. Why don't we contact some outside guild, some outside union carpenter who, for a fee, will come and fix the door. You can take it out of my entertainment allowance. *(Silence.)* Why don't we do that?

Adam: Because this is a landmark building. Because we have a maintenance department right here in the co-op which does all the work for free. And because they are the only ones who are authorized to make repairs of any kind. It's all in the bylaws in our housing handbook which you refuse to read. Does that answer your question?

Dianne: Yes.

Adam: Any other questions?

Dianne: No. But I do have a comment. Perhaps if the maintenance department of this co-op were not entirely staffed with handymen who're all famous Wagnerian tenors then perhaps we could have the door fixed.

Adam: I told you from the start that everyone here is an artist.

Dianne: You didn't tell me that the super and the maintenance people were.

Adam: I said everyone. Everyone means everyone. And they're not famous Wagnerian tenors. They're up and coming Wagnerian tenors. That's why they are still in the maintenance department. Any other comments?

Dianne: No. But I do have an exclamation.

Adam: If you must.

Dianne: I don't know if I must, but I'd sure like to.

Adam: Go ahead.

Dianne: I know how you feel about gutter language, so please consider the following expletives deleted ahead of time. *(Takes a beat. A deep breath.)* Fuck this place! Fuck this co-op! Fuck the housing handbook! Fuck the maintenance department! FUCK THAT MOTHER-FUCKING DOOR!

She jumps up and grabs one of the huge stuffed animals, a huge bear perhaps, and starts dragging it toward the door. It's not easy. She drags it to the door. She shuts the door. She holds it shut with her foot. She drags the animal to rest against the door. She's out of breath. She waits. It seems to work. Lights dim.

Thank God for toys.

She is ready to return to her place, but she stands there. Looks up and around as if wondering about something. Rubs her eyes.

Did a bunch of lightbulbs blow or am I going blind or what?

Adam: It's central lighting.

Dianne: Oh, yeah. I keep forgetting.

She looks up and around. Ready to curse. He cuts her off.

Adam: Please don't.

Dianne: *(She mimes the words:)* Fuck the lighting. *(Smiles. Tries to be pleasant. Out loud:)* It's nice how it changes without you having to do anything. *(Sighs.)*

Adam: Are you going dressed like that?

Dianne: Going where?

Adam: It's Saturday. They're showing a movie in the rec room downstairs.

Dianne: I'm not going.

Adam: Everyone's going. That couple upstairs. They're in it.

Dianne: I don't like horror movies.

Adam: It's not a horror movie.

Dianne: Does it have music?

Adam: Of course it has music. The man downstairs wrote it.

Dianne: I'm not going. *(She sits down.)* What's it called? You know, when they have music in a movie.

Adam: Movie music.

Dianne: There's a name.

Adam: The score.

Dianne: That's it. The score. I can't bear those movies where some poor guy doesn't know the score. You know. You see a movie and there's some poor guy just sitting at home minding his own business, thinking his thoughts . . .

Adam: Man sitting at home thinking his thoughts.

Sounds like a blockbuster.

Dianne: All right. He's at home with his wife or mistress or lover and they're giggling and exchanging pleasantries. He's planning a ski vacation to Switzerland. He's feeling wonderful. But all the time there's this music playing. There's this music that we can hear but that he can't. And this music is telling us that there's a man waiting in the garage ready to plunge a knife into his heart. The music tells us that the woman he's with, the one he thinks he's taking on his ski vacation, is in on the scheme. She knows about the man in the garage. She knows about the knife. She's in on the betrayal. Everyone's in on it except the poor guy in question because everyone can hear the music except for him. All he hears are the words being spoken.

Adam: I know this movie. There's no knives. Nobody gets murdered. It's a love story.

Dianne: I've seen one of those. This couple falls in love and then they go shopping. They go shopping while the music plays. What's that called when they run around in a movie and live life to the hilt while the music plays?

Adam: A montage.

Dianne: That's it. They're both in this montage where time passes and music plays. They have kids. One second, the kids are tiny. The next, they're old enough to go shopping by themselves. The next, they're leaving home to start a montage of their own. Moments of life appear. Disappear. Their lives fly by like Christmas cards. The montage machine is making mincemeat of them all but they don't mind. They're happy. They smile. Time passes. Music plays. It's worse than murder.

Adam: Have it your way. I'll see you later. *(Starts to go.)*

Dianne: Don't go. Why don't we stay together for once?

Adam: We've been together the whole day.

Dianne: We have?

Adam: The whole day.

Dianne: Really?

Adam: All to ourselves.

Dianne: Just stand there for a moment. Let me look at you. And you look at me. Let us try and fix one another in our minds and then when time starts rushing by again we can hold on to what we see in each other now. All right?

Adam: All right.

Blackout.

Scene Two

In the darkness music plays. Lights up their apartment. Same as before. The huge stuffed animal is still holding the door shut. The others are as before. Adam is sitting. Looks up. Thinks. Performs a dramatic hand gesture, mouthing some words. Thinks. Does it all again, but different emphasis, slightly different gesture. Mouths words, giving a silent but very dramatic reading of something. Dianne *is extremely pregnant sitting in the rocking chair. She sees Adam doing his stuff. Looks at him for a beat or two. She looks at Adam. He's doing what he was doing before: silent but dramatic reading of something.*

Adam *turns toward her.*

Adam: Which do you like better?

Dianne *thinks a bit, as she rocks in her chair.*

Dianne: What?

Adam: With or without? What do you think?

Dianne: With or without what?

Adam: Weren't you paying attention?

Dianne: I thought I was. I must have drifted off. But I'm all yours now.

Adam *does a bit from the part he's been rehearsing.*

Adam: Where do we go from here? Where do you want to go? *(A beat.)* Or: Where do we go from here? *(Gestures to her.)* Where do you want to go? *(A beat.)* So? Which one do you like better?

Dianne: They're both delightful.

Adam: With or without the gesture? What do you think?

Dianne: It's a shame you can't have both.

Adam: One or the other.

Dianne: The other.

Adam: Without?

Dianne: Yes.

Adam: That's what I thought.

Dianne: This may strike you as silly.

Adam: What?

Dianne: I have a personal problem I'd like to . . .

Adam: In a minute. I promise. I have to videotape this today, to make sure it gets submitted before the deadline. Thousands are applying. And out of those thousands do you know how many will actually be picked to deliver the president's ultimatum to the country?

Dianne: I think you told me, but I forgot.

Adam: Only seventeen hundred. One for every major TV market outlet. I could be one of the seventeen hundred.

Dianne: In my book, you already are.

Adam: Thank you. *(Refers to the pages in his hand.)* Now. This. This to me is the crucial part. You've known me a long time and . . . *(Takes a beat and begins. First reading is declamatory, flat.)*You all know what you'd be getting with me. Or: *(Conspiratory.)* You all know what you'd be getting with me. Or: *(Cynical.)* You all know what you'd be getting with me. Or: *(Sexy, seductive.)* You all know what you'd be getting with me. Or: *(Threatening.)* You all know what you'd be getting with me. Or: *(Chummy.)* You all know what you'd be getting with me. Or: *(Faustian.)* You all know what you'd be getting with me. Or: *(Disarming.)* You all know what you'd be getting with me. Or: *(Spaeaking to thousands.)* YOU ALL KNOW WHAT YOU'D BE GETTING WITH ME. Or: *(Speaking just to you.)* You all know what you'd be getting with me. *(Stops. Waits for comment from her.)* Well?

Dianne: They're all exquisite.

Adam: Which one did you like best?

Dianne: I didn't like any of them at all, but they're all superb.

Adam: I need your opinion. I really do. Pick your favorite.

She's wracking her brains.

I'll do them all once again.

He's ready to start. She's desperate he shouldn't.

Dianne: Four!

Adam: Really? *(He does number four: sexy.)* You all know what you'd be getting with me. That one?

Dianne: Yes!

Adam: I think your're right. *(Looks at his watch.)* I better get going.

Dianne: Wait. What about me?

He stops.

Personal problem. Remember?

He snaps his fingers and whacks himself on the head.

Adam: I'm sorry. *(Takes a step toward her. Stops.)* You have a problem.

Dianne: Yes.

Adam: What is it?

She stands up, but holds on to the chair.

Dianne: I'm pregnant.

He waits. Looks at his watch.

Adam: What is it? You can tell me.

Dianne: I'm pregnant.

He looks her over.

Adam: What do you mean, you're pregnant?

Dianne: That's exactly what I mean.

Adam: What're you trying to tell me?

Dianne: Me woman. Me have womb. Baby in womb. Soon baby go from womb to baby room.

Adam: I don't understand.

Dianne: I don't either. How did it happen?

Adam: You're not being serious, are you?

Dianne: Of course I'm serious. You think I'm kidding? I'm pregnant, I tell you.

Adam: Of course you're pregnant!

Dianne: How did it happen?

Adam: It didn't just happen. You've been pregnant for months and months.

Dianne: I know that. I'm not an idiot, you know. But I was standing over there, if my memory serves me right, telling you, for a variety of reasons which I can't remember now, but telling you in no uncertain terms that I was against the idea of bringing a little one into this world at this time. It all seems so recent. Like it all happened yesterday. Today. An hour ago. Less. But I remember standing there, right there, and I remember standing tough. I remember being firm in my decision. Full of convictions.

Adam: I remember that, too. You were splendid. What's the problem?

Dianne: I don't remember changing my mind. What happened to my convictions? There's something about this co-op that makes it hard for me to keep track of myself. There's music playing. And when it's not playing, I'm waiting for it to start again. There's these lights. They seem to have a life of their own. (*She gestures around, up at the lights, back at herself.*) I know. I shouldn't blame the place. But being the way I am, I'm desperate for an excuse. I just can't get over how it all happened without me, I don't know. Without me. It worries me this kind of behavior. I was against this . . . (*Alludes to her pregnancy.*) But now that it's here inside of me, I'm for it but it worries me. If I could accept it without a struggle, I might lose it in the same way.

Adam: Now I understand. You think you changed your mind on this issue without putting up a fight?

Dianne: I don't remember putting up a fight, no.

Adam: Are you kidding?

Dianne: No. Why? Did I put up a fight?

Adam: Did you? Did you ever! I hope to tell you did.

She would hear more.

Dianne: Oh, yeah?

Adam: You were a wildcat. A wildcat.

Dianne: Really? I fought back?

Adam: Did you? Did the Spartans fight back at Thermopylae? Did King Lazar and the Serbians fight back at Kossovo? Tooth and nail you fought me on this one.

Dianne: Oh, yeah?

Adam: Tooth and nail, I tell you. You wouldn't budge. Not an inch.

She's too caught up in enjoying his description of her glorious struggle.

Do you want to hear what you said to me when I tried to push you to go against yourself?

Dianne: I'd pay admission to hear it.

Adam: All right. Here I go. This is you, speaking. And I'm quoting you. Verbatim: "There are times when the only thing one can do, the only freedom one has left is the freedom of non-compliance. The freedom to say I will produce no more life until the life that's already here is respected and cherished the way it should be. And when that time comes I will glady blossom and bear fruit." End of quote.

Dianne: I said that?

Adam: And not just once either.

Dianne: It's amazing I lost.

Adam: Amazing nothing. It was a miracle.

Dianne: It's good to know I didn't just cave in.

Adam: You? Never. *(Checks his watch.)* I gotta go now. *(Starts to go. Points back at her.)* A wildcat.

He exits. She watches him go, still somewhat under the influence of her heroic but forgotten past. Playfully puffed up and full of herself. The lights are changing. She's looking up at them as she sits. Piano plays.

Blackout.

Scene Three

Lights up. An image is required to tell us that what we're seeing is either being transmitted or actually seen on television. Adam's wearing a suit and tie. He walks up to his mark and stops. He waits, a bit nervous, for a signal to start. He gets the signal. He starts.

Adam: Good evening. It is now nine o'clock and it is prime time in our nation. But it won't stay prime time for long. So the question before us now is this: It is prime time for what? To take stock of ourselves? To stop and take stock of who we are and where we've been and what turns we took in the road that lead us to where we are today? The facts are these. The turns have been taken. We are where we are today because the turns have been taken and there is no turning back. The question is not how we got to where we are, but where do we go from here. We've had integration, then disintegration, and now reconstructive reintegration, but where do we go from here? We've had days of division then days of vision and now we have a revision of that vision, but where do we go from here? Where do you want to go? Do you know? Do you have any idea? Do you care one way or another? If you don't care one way or another, don't be ashamed to admit it. You don't have to pretend with me because I'm not pretending with you. We are only human after all and we all know what that means. We only want what's best for ourselves and we all know what that means. Some of us know what's best for our nation and if confirmed I promise to tell you what that means. If I'm not confirmed I can't promise anything. You've known me a long time, and you all know what you'd be getting with me. You've been getting it all these years and you'll get more if I'm confirmed. If I'm not confirmed, I can't promise who'll get what. Maybe you'll get yours and then maybe you won't. If I'm confirmed and things go wrong you won't have yourselves to blame. That's my job. But if I'm not confirmed I can't promise where the blame might fall. I have only one plank on my platform. Others talk about freedom. I do something about it. This is a referendum for our future. Telephone numbers are flashing on your TV screens right now. There is one for my confirmation and there is one against and there is yet a third for a tyrant of your choice. Operators are standing by to take your call. Good night and God bless you.

Blackout.

Scene Four

In the darkness, we hear a baby cry out. Once, twice, three times. Silence. Lights up. Their apartment. Dianne is sitting in the rocking chair. Adam is standing and waiting impatiently. Dianne looks up at him. Shrugs helplessly. Looks away.

Adam: You saw the show, right? Well? So?

Dianne: I'm trying to think.

Adam: What's there to think about? I'm just asking you what you thought of the show, the speech. You must know what you thought of it.

Dianne: You would think so, yes.

She wracks her brains. He waits.

Adam: This is very cruel of you.

Dianne: All right. I've got it. *(She turns slightly and assumes a posture of someone who has an opinion to give. She looks lost.)* It was a real eye-opener. A tour de force. It was brash and irreverant. Made you sit up and listen. Made you stop and think. It made all those past shows look like a picnic in the park. A clambake. A brunch. It made mincemeat out of them. It never lapsed into sentimentality. It was disturbing. It was what it was. That was one of its strengths. It knew what it was. It wasn't afraid to be what it was. There was no hope in it, but then it wasn't about hope. It knew what it was about. Made no bones about it. Made no apologies for itself. Made you sit up and look. Made you lean back and wonder. It had its own voice. A voice for our time. A timeless voice. It demanded to be heard. It grabbed you by the throat and wouldn't let go. *(She stops, out of breath.)*

Adam: You're not just saying that, are you?

Dianne: I don't know.

Adam: I'm so glad you liked it.

Dianne: I never said I liked it. You never asked me if I liked it.

Silence. Adam *waits. She rocks the baby.* Adam *waits.*

Adam: Well? Did you like it or didn't you?

Dianne: Now that you mention it, I didn't.

Adam: You didn't?

Dianne: I don't think so.

Adam: You didn't hate it, did you?

Dianne: Now that you mention it, I did.

Adam: You hated it?

Dianne: Yes, quite a bit. I tend to hate that particular . . . what's that word?

Adam: *Genre.*

Dianne: That's it. I hate that *genre.*

Adam: What's wrong with the *genre?*

Dianne: I didn't say there was anything wrong with the *genre.* Per se. But these tyrannical ultimatums. They're old hat. I've seen them before. I've heard them before. I hate them.

Adam: Of course you've seen them before and heard them before. We weren't trying to do something new and different. That wasn't the point. It was an old-fashioned tyrannical ultimatum pure and simple. Call it a revival. That's all we were doing. A revival.

Dianne: Maybe I hate revivals.

Adam: Maybe you don't understand revivals!

Dianne: Maybe you don't understand hatred! *(A beat.)*

Adam: All right. All right. *Genre* aside, what did you think of my performance?

Dianne: I don't know if what you had to say was my idea of a good time.

Adam: Forget what I said! I didn't write the damned thing. What did you think of the way I said it?

Dianne: I've heard it all before.

He's beside himself.

Adam: Of course you've heard it all before. It was a revival! A revival! Don't you get it? How many times do I have to say it? It was a revival.

Dianne: Call it what you will. I hated it. And hating something is not my idea of a good time.

Adam: You wouldn't know a good time if it hit you right between the eyes.

Dianne: I may not know anymore what I love or what I like, but I still know what I hate. And I hated it.

Adam: It really affected you in a very profound way, didn't it?

Dianne: Yes, it did.

Adam: Well, then. All was not lost. At least you were entertained.

Dianne: No, I wasn't. I hated it.

Adam: The two are not incompatible. I've seen it happen a lot in my line of work. People get confused. Thet think their hatred or opposition to something is bound to keep them from being entertained. It's not. That's not how this business works. Nobody knows for sure how it works. That's the magic of it.

Her moment of certainty is fading. She's trying to hold on to it. He sees. Softens.

Adam: It's always a shock the first time it happens. I went through it myself. The exact same thing. I was just a kid when it happened and if you think you're shocked to discover that you were entertained this evening, you should've seen me then. I was so young, I didn't know what hit me. I was so young, I still believed there was right and wrong and all the rest of it. Well, you can imagine how I felt when I discovered that I was entertained and entertained in a very meaningful way by everything that I thought was deplorable and downright sinister. I guess in the end that's what attracted me to this line of work.

Silence. Two, three beats and then the Baby *cries out.* Dianne *gets up with the baby. Crying stops. The door opens. A light comes on like a light in a fridge. She goes inside the baby room. She comes out. The door shuts gently. Heads to the bedroom. Goes inside the bedroom. The door shuts.* Adam *stands where he stood. Silence. It lasts just enough to be almost too long and then suddenly and simultaneously two things happen. The door to the baby room blows open and the baby's crying is heard loud and piercing.* Adam *listens to it and then he walks to the door. Shuts it. The crying either ceases or we can't hear it with the door shut.*

Blackout.

Scene Five

Adam on the Patriotic Variety Hour. He sings.

Patriotism has gone out of fashion,
We seem to think our patriotic days are dead,
We used to sing of our homeland with passion,
But now we seem to shy away from it instead.
I think it's time we hit the nail right on the head.

This is a great country,
A great country,
So let's shout it clear and loud,
Take a look in your history book,
And you'll see why we should be proud.

Repeats verse half talking-half singing.

Hats off to this land of ours,
The home of the free and the brave.
If this is flag waving, flag waving,
Do you know a better flag to wave?

Repeats verse building for a finale.

Blackout.

Scene Six

In the darkness we hear a baby crying. It cries once. Twice. Three times. There's a beat of silence. And then it goes on crying. Its voice no longer has the strength it once had. It's now weak and pitiful and pleading. Lights up, their apartment. Dianne is sitting on the floor with the baby in her arms. Adam is sitting in his chair. The huge stuffed animals are as they were. The baby cries.

Dianne: Oh, baby.

It cries. Adam paces around her.

My poor baby.

It cries.

My poor little baby.

It cries.

Oh, baby.

Adam: You mustn't.

Dianne: Isn't there anything we can do?

Adam: No.

Dianne: Nothing?

Adam: Nothing whatsoever.

Dianne: It's dying.

Adam: One can never be sure. But there's nothing we can do. All we can do is wait for the crisis to pass.

Dianne: That's all?

Adam: Yes.

Dianne: But it's dying.

Adam: You've read the literature. All we can do is let nature take its course.

Dianne cries out.

You mustn't torture yourself like that. It does no good. You don't have to prove anything to me. I know exactly how you feel, because I feel the same way. Just because we don't flaunt our agony the way they used to doesn't mean it's not there. Our humanity's our own affair. We don't have to prove it to anybody.

The baby's cry rises a bit. Subsides.

At least . . .

It rises again. He waits for it to subside.

At least, if nothing else, this poor little thing can give voice to its torment. Whereas I, we, we have to bear ours in silence. And how much harder that is. How much more persuasive. And you mustn't forget . . .

The crying rises again. He waits for it to subside. It doesn't. He raises his voice to ride over it.

You mustn't ever forget that we don't really know for sure that the poor little thing is in any pain at all. You've read the literature, the journals, the brochures, the copyrighted stories. Written by authorities on the subject of suffering and pain. And all of them concur that in cases such as this, there is no suffering to speak of. As a matter of fact . . .

The baby's crying subsides and so does his voice.

As a matter of fact, they suspect just the opposite. They suspect that in cases such as this there is a state of acceptance. A state of numbness that's not really a numbness but a kind of peace. But no suffering to speak of. No pain to speak of. I know, I realize, to you, to me, to us, to any layman what we're hearing now sounds very much like suffering but that's because we've been conditioned to interpret it in a certain way, whereas the truth, according to all the data on hand, points in just the opposite direction.

Dianne: I know. I've read the literature.

Adam: Not all the literature.

Dianne: No, not all.

It cries very weakly now.

My poor little baby. What can I do?

Adam: If you had read all the literature, the periodicals, the weeklies, the monthlies, the quarterlies, you would know that there is nothing you can do. Not in cases such as this. Actually, they warn against trying. Nine times out of ten, and here I'm quoting, nine times out of ten, you can do more harm than good.

The crying is fading.

Dianne: It's looking at me. Such large eyes for one so small.

Adam: If it's any comfort to you it really can't see you. In cases such as this, the eyes stay open, but they see nothing anymore. It's all peaceful and dark.

The crying stops. Silence.

Dianne: It's gone!

She seems intent on just sitting there with the baby in her arms, weeping, keening, but Adam, *gently and solicitously, gets her to stand and leads her toward the baby room. He opens the door for her. She goes inside. He waits outside. One beat. Two beats.*

Three beats. She comes out, grief-stricken and emptyhanded. Crosses to bedroom. Exits. Adam *stands there.*

Blackout.

Scene Seven

In the darkness we hear the sound of a mighty vacuum cleaner. Lights up. Dianne *is sitting in the rocking chair with the vacuum roaring next to her. She seems in a trance. All the huge stuffed animals are gone. Enter* Adam. *He's wearing a black arm band around the sleeve of his jacket.* Dianne *turns. Sees him. Shuts off the vacuum cleaner.*

Adam: It's really too bad you refused to come. It was really something. It really was.

Dianne: I suppose everyone was there.

Adam: To the last tenant. Except for you, which is ironic seeing as how it was all done ... *(He gestures toward her.)*

Dianne: I just couldn't.

She exits with vacuum cleaner and returns in the middle of his speech.

Adam: They were all there. And they had all worked so hard. The singers from the co-op had formed a choir. The musicians an orchestra. And all of them were brought together for the single purpose of paying a tribute to the loss of our little loved one. It was all so poignant, so moving. And as the super said to me, it was as if our loss were a catalyst which brought everyone together so that we weren't just thousands of tenants anymore but a big family. In all his years here, he said, he had never seen anything like it.

Dianne: And they sang and played their various instruments?

Adam: Verdi's Requiem.

Dianne: That's one of the good ones, isn't it?

Adam: It was transporting. They were all inspired, that's all I can say. Inspired in the true sense of that word. And seeing all those people from the East and West Wings of the co-op brought together by our loss made me feel better. Made me feel that maybe the poor little thing didn't die for nothing. It was overwhelming.

Dianne: I'm glad you had a good time and I hope you explained to them why I couldn't come.

Adam: I tried. But I think they felt hurt.

Dianne: I'm still huting myself. In my own way.

Adam: Of course you are. But that was the whole point of this event. To help you get over it.

Dianne: I'm sure they meant well.

Adam: Of course they meant well.

Dianne: I'm sure they did. But . . . I don't know. Maybe it's just me, maybe it's this place, but I have enough problems as it is holding on to . . . things . . . without anyone trying to help me get over them or whatever the hell it is they want from me.

Adam: Surely you're not questioning their sincerity.

Dianne: Oh, no. Not me. If they're anything, they're

sincere. I've never been around such vigorous sincerity in all my life. It's a living nightmare trying to live around it.

Adam: And what's that supposed to mean?

Dianne: I wish I were smarter. I wish I were a lot smarter. I mean I wish I were brilliant because then I could explain what I mean. One thing's for sure: You don't want to have a nosebleed around a bunch of sharks.

Adam: That's a stupid thing to say. I don't know what you mean by that, but that's a very stupid thing to say.

Dianne: That's part of my problem. I'm so stupid it would take a genius to explain what I mean. And I'm no genius. So all I can tell you is what I'm telling you. Let me put it this way: I gave birth to a little bit of new life and it died. I'm not inspired by that loss. I don't feel inspired by it at all. But they're all inspired by it.

Adam: They're all artists. That's their job.

Dianne: I know. But whay don't they pick on somebody else?

Adam: They're not picking on you. You don't understand anything. You ever hear of empathy?

Dianne: I've heard of it.

Adam: It was a collective expression of empathy.

Dianne: I'm sure they meant well.

Adam: Of course they meant well.

Dianne: I'm sure they did. But . . . let me put it another way. Jesus Christ returns to earth. For whatever reason, call it faulty navigation, he makes a big mistake and lands on a continent inhabited by cannibals. Religious cannibals. Christian cannibals. And in their fervor to worship him they proceed to eat His flesh and drink His blood and poof. . . He's all gone. All I'm saying is this: You wouldn't call that a Holy Communion. Nor would you call them insincere.

Adam: I don't know what you're trying to tell me.

Dianne: I want out.

Adam: What do you mean out?

Dianne: I mean out. Out of here. Out of this. Out of all this. I see no other way. I hate to spring this on you, but I want a divorce.

Adam: A divorce?

She just gestures.

You want a divorce?

She nods and gestures again.

But why?

Dianne: Oh, please. If I had to explain, this marriage would last forever and I want a divorce.

Adam: After all we've been through?

Dianne: And before we go through any more. And while I still have some grasp on the things that matter, yes.

Adam: But what about our little one?

Dianne: It died, Mister.

Adam: That's what I mean. Are we to say that it died for nothing?

Dianne: I hope not.

Adam: Are we to say that the tragedy we suffered was suffered for nothing? Don't you see? We can use this tragedy. And I'm not just speaking as an artist now. I'm speaking as a human being. This tragedy can make us stronger, bring us closer together and become a spring-board for spiritual growth.

Dianne: That's what I'm afraid of. That's another reason I want out while there's still time. I want a divorce from a way of life in which constant processions of tragedies and sacrifices of innocents are required just so that we can grow as human beings. It might become addictive. So . . .

She gestures and heads toward him with an outstretched hand of farewell. But suddenly she hears, as we do, the co-op symphony orchestra and choir doing a section of Verdi's "Requiem" outside their window. She is stunned. She looks around.

What the hell is that?

Adam *knows and gestures.*

Adam: Look.

She comes and looks. She's horrified.

You wouldn't come to them so they've come to you. It means that much to them.

The voices rise louder and louder, the music fuller and fuller, Dianne is more and more horrified. Dianne is backing away as the beautiful music builds. Backs up to main door. Blackout. In the darkness, the Verdi's "Requiem" continues until the conclusion of that section.

Scene Eight

The park. A bench. Sitting on the bench is Dianne. *She is wearing glasses. She just sits there looking out at us. Enter* Adam. *He enters on a diagonal and can see her from the back without her seeing him. He's carrying a bag of snacks he's eating. He stops. Looks at her. Consideres what to do. Decides not to make contact. Starts to exit. Stops. Checks his watch. Heads toward her. She feels him approaching. Turns. They see each other. Both smile in their own ways. He stops next to her.*

Adam: Do you mind if I join you?

Dianne: Yes, I do. But please . . .   *(She gestures an invitation.)*

Adam: Thank you. *(Sits down. A beat of silence. He offers his bag.)* Care for a bonbon?

She looks at the bag. Looks inside. Takes one.

Dianne: Thank you.

She eats it. He eats his. She signifies it tastes good.

Adam: It's been a while.

Dianne: I'll say.

Adam: *(A tiny beat.)* You look . . . *(He gestures a compliment.)*

Dianne: And you seem . . . *(She gestures one back.)*

Adam: All things considered, I think we're both . . . *(Another gesture.)* Glasses, eh?

Dianne: Yes. What can you do?

Adam: They look good on you.

Dianne: It's like wearing a little bicycle without a rider. Sometimes just seeing clearly feels like a form of transportation. *(She laughs.)*

Adam: What?

Dianne: Nothing. *(Laughs.)* A silly game I sometimes play. *(Laughs.)*

Adam: What?

Dianne: Well. I pretend every now and then that some little person hops on my bicycle *(She puts her finger in the seat of the glasses to demonstrate.)* and this little person likes to play tour guide. This little person likes to tell me where we're going next and what it is I'm seeing. Well. It's ever so much fun to just go . . . *(Shakes her head.)* Knock him off my face.

Looks down on the ground at the fallen rider.

Sorry about that. *(Laughs.)* They keep coming and I keep knocking 'em off. Speaking of which. How're you doing?

He takes a pleasant beat and holds up two fingers. She looks at the victory sign.

Don't tell me. You made it! You made the grade. You're second class.

He can't hide his pride despite the show of modesty.

I knew you could do it. Congratulations.

Adam: Thank you. You always had faith in me.

Dianne: No, I never had any faith in you at all. But I knew you would do whatever it took.

In the distance we hear the first faint sound of parade music. Drums.

Dianne: What's going on?

Adam: Don't tell me you don't know what today is?

Dianne *thinks. A wild guess.*

Dianne: Wednesday?

Adam: It's Friday, but that's beside the point. The point is . . .

Dianne: It's Friday? Really?

Adam: Yes, but . . .

Dianne: How about that?

Adam: That's not the point. The point is it's a national holiday.

Dianne: The start of the weekend?

Adam: No. It's the semi-annual National Victory Day.

Dianne: Today?

Adam: That's right.

Dianne: National Victory Day?

Adam: That's right. The whole country's celebrating.

Dianne: What kind of victory?

Adam: A decisive victory.

Dianne: Over what?

Adam: Over the fact that it was all worth it. All the sacrifices and everything. Reconstruction is over.

Dianne: Today?

Adam: No, it officially ended a while ago, but today was the day that was picked to celebrate. Where have you been?

She laughs.

Dianne: That's a good question.

He checks his watch.

Adam: There's going to be a parade, pageants, unveiling of statues and commemorative plaques. I hope you're coming.

Dianne: I don't think so.

Silence.

Adam: Crême brulée! Remember?

Both laugh.

You were so heartbroken and looked so betrayed when you discovered there was no crême brulée.

Dianne: I felt betrayed. *(But she's laughing.)* I was betrayed. *(She's smiling.)* I should've known right then and there. *(A beat.)* Youth.

Adam: Not a day goes by . . . well. It's hard to be exact. To be on the safe side of truth I'll say a week. Not a week goes by . . . *(Stops.)* It was on this very bench wasn't it, that we . . . *(He gestures, alluding to their former union.)*

Dianne: Yes. It was a Wednesday afternoon. Moments are born. Sometimes in solitude. Sometimes between a couple in the park. Newborn moments that are almost as lovely as newborn babes. Almost as lovely.

Adam: I remember.

Dianne: All I remember are their births and their aftermaths. The inbetweens are lost. None of them lived long enough to link together. Or if they did, I can't recall.

Adam: It's not easy. We're only human after all.

Dianne: It's like there are tunnels. We take our lovely newborn moments and set out on our journeys full of love. Full of life. And before we know it there it is. The dreadful dark tunnel awaits. And in the tunnel, the tyrant of our choice. He says nothing. Makes no demands. We know what to do. We hand them over. Our treasures. Our newborn moments. Here. We pay the toll so we don't have to go through the darkness ourselves. We get to walk around in the light and when we reach the other side our moments are there waiting for us. The living marrow has been sucked from their bones. The bones are dead and hollow and when we hit one against the other they resonate and make a lovely life-like sound. The sound is music to our ears and makes us forget what we lost. We beat our dead bones and continue our journey. Time passes. Music plays.

Adam: But life goes on.

Dianne: Yes.

Silence. They look at each other and then she looks away. A beat and then Adam *starts to sing softly the love song he sang to her in Act I. They're both moved by it. He does not manage to sing the whole thing. Just enough to bring it all back. Then he stops.*

Dianne: Your voice is lovelier than ever. It's heart-breaking.

Adam: Thank you.

Dianne: What's it called when you sing like that?

Adam: Remorse, I think.

Dianne: When you sing without music. There's a name for it.

Adam: A cappella.

Dianne: That's right. *(She loves the sound of it as she says it herself.)* A cappella! What a thing.

In the distance, we hear the sound of parade music. Drums. Adam reacts to it. Checks his watch. Alludes to it.

I know.

He rises. Starts to go. Stops.

Adam: I don't supose you . . . *(Gestures toward the parade.)*

Dianne: No, thank you.

He waits. Something else on his mind.

Adam: I don't suppose . . . *(His gesture unites them into a couple.)*

Dianne: No.

Adam: I didn't think so.

Starts to go. Stops, despite the pressure of time that he's feeling.

I have to say this. You gave me so much. It'll always be with me. Thank you.

Dianne: And thank you for overlooking how much more I had to give.

The drumming grows. He feels the pressure to leave. He looks at his watch and gestures to her, excusing his departure. Walks away. Stops. The drumming grows. He looks toward the music and then quickly towrd her.

Adam: You mustn't stay there, you know.

Dianne: I know. I can hear the music.

Adam: Good-bye.

Dianne: Good-bye.

Adam *rushes away, exiting. The drumming grows.* Dianne *sits still and erect. The drumming grows. She rises as if afraid, as if ready to leave, but then all she does is adjust the wrinkled dress under her fanny and sits down again. More erect than ever. The drums are drumming louder and closer. Lights are fading. She adjusts her glasses and stares at the approaching darkness. The drums grow louder and louder and louder. Faster and faster rhythm. And then suddenly they stop.*

Blackout.

The End